Great Inventions

THE CAMERA

by Larry Hills

Consultant:
Michelle Delaney
Museum Specialist/Collections Manager
Photographic History Collection
National Museum of American History
Smithsonian Institution, Washington, D.C.

Capstone press®

Mankato, Minnesota

Fact Finders is published by Capstone Press,
151 Good Counsel Drive, P.O. Box 669, Mankato, Minnesota 56002.
www.capstonepress.com

Library of Congress Cataloging-in-Publication Data
Hills, Larry.
    The camera / Larry Hills.
    p. cm.—(Fact finders. Great inventions)
    Includes bibliographical references and index.
    ISBN-13: 978-0-7368-2669-3 (hardcover)   ISBN-10: 0-7368-2669-6 (hardcover)
    ISBN-13: 978-0-7368-4724-7 (softcover pbk.) ISBN-10: 0-7368-4724-3 (softcover pbk.)
    1. Cameras—History—Juvenile literature. [1. Cameras—History. 2. Inventions.]
I. Title. II. Series.
TR250.H52 2005
771.3—dc22
                           2003026087

Summary: Introduces the history and development of the camera and explains how a film
    camera works.

Editorial Credits
Christopher Harbo, editor; Juliette Peters, series designer; Patrick Dentinger, book designer
    and illustrator; Kelly Garvin, photo researcher; Eric Kudalis, product planning editor

Photo Credits
Bayerisches National Museum, 4–5
Capstone Press/Gary Sundermeyer, 24–25, 27 (all)
Corbis, 6–7; Bettmann, 8, 14–15, 17, 18; Michael Freeman, 12, 26 (left)
Getty Images/Hulton Archive, 10–11, 13
Ingram Publishing, 1
Leica Camera AG, 19
Mary Evans Picture Library, 9
Photo by David Hoyt, 20, 21
Photo by Larry S. Pierce, 26 (middle)
Stockbyte, cover, 26 (right)

Artistic Effects
Corbis, 25 (background)

1 2 3 4 5 6 09 08 07 06 05 04

Table of Contents

Chapter 1

Science Meets Art

In 1839, an unlikely group of people gathered in Paris, France. The country's top scientists met with its most famous artists. The scientists and artists hardly knew each other.

Louis Jacques Mandé Daguerre was the main speaker at the meeting. Daguerre was not a scientist or an artist. He was an entertainer. He had earned a fortune through his popular **dioramas**. These giant paintings showed events from history and literature. They were lit from behind to create stunning effects.

▲ This 1838 photograph by Louis Daguerre shows buildings and trees along a street in Paris, France.

Daguerre amazed the artists and scientists with a new kind of picture. He showed them pictures made with light. It was the first time these people saw photographs.

Chapter 2

Before the Camera

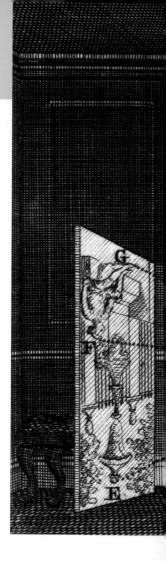

Pictures have been around for thousands of years. Early people drew pictures of animals and hunters on cave walls. People later painted and sculpted what they thought was important.

Camera Obscura

Early artists searched for ways to make their art look real. The ancient Greeks found a way to make an image with light. They used a tool called the **camera obscura**. This term means darkened room in Latin.

▲ In this early camera obscura, light passed through a small hole into a large dark room. Pictures made by the light appeared upside down and backward.

An artist uses a camera obscura to trace pictures of the real world.

A camera obscura let light enter a dark room through a tiny hole. The light hit the wall opposite the tiny hole. The light formed an image of the outside scene on the wall. The image appeared upside down and backward.

Some artists used the camera obscura to trace images of their subjects. Tracing helped artists paint pictures that looked more like their subjects.

Over time, the camera obscura box was made small enough for people to carry. In 1558, Giambattista della Porta put a lens in a camera obscura. The lens made images sharper and brighter. Artists also added mirrors to show images right side up.

Photochemicals

Scientists also took steps toward the invention of the camera. In 1727, German scientist Johann Heinrich Schultz discovered **photochemicals**. He found that a solution of silver and salt turned dark in sunlight. Other scientists soon tested photochemicals.

This camera obscura at a park was large enough for several ▼ people to stand inside.

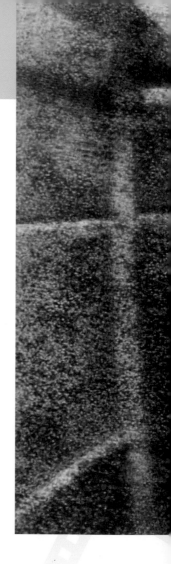

Chapter 3

Inventors

The camera was not invented by just one person. Many people invented ways to capture images. Their early cameras changed the way people saw the world.

Niepce and Daguerre

In the 1820s, Joseph N. Niepce from France tried to capture an image with light. In 1827, he coated a metal plate with a light-sensitive material. He put the plate in a camera obscura box. Niepce let light shine on the plate for eight hours. The plate recorded the scene outside his window. Niepce called his picture a heliograph.

▲ Joseph Niepce's first picture showed a view of the buildings and field outside his window.

That same year, Niepce met Louis Daguerre. Daguerre liked Niepce's heliographs. Niepce and Daguerre worked together to make better heliographs. After Niepce died in 1833, Daguerre continued the work.

In 1837, Daguerre invented the daguerreotype camera. He used a mixture of silver and iodine to capture images on copper plates. His camera made clear black and white images. But Daguerre's images had one drawback. No one could make copies of them.

The daguerreotype camera was a small wood box with a lens on the front.

William Henry Fox Talbot

In 1839, William Henry Fox Talbot from England invented the calotype camera. The calotype made **negative images** on paper. These images show light areas as dark and dark areas as light. Talbot shined light through the negative image to make a positive image.

Talbot could make many copies of calotype pictures. But the pictures were not as clear as daguerreotype pictures. People continued to look for ways to make better pictures.

▲ William Henry Fox Talbot holds part of his calotype camera.

FACT!

In 1844, William Talbot published *The Pencil of Nature*. It was the first book illustrated with photographs.

Wet Plates and Dry Plates

In 1851, an English inventor named Frederick Archer captured images on glass plates. He covered the plates with a wet chemical mixture called **collodion**. Wet plates allowed him to make copies of a picture.

Wet plates were messy. The sticky collodion had to be used wet. If it dried, the picture would not turn out. Photographers also had to develop the pictures right after they were taken.

Civil War (1860–1864) photographers developed their pictures in tentlike darkrooms near battlefields. ➤

14

In the 1880s, Dr. Richard Maddox from England invented dry plates. These plates used a coating of **gelatin** and other chemicals. Unlike collodion, the gelatin could be used dry. Dry plates were not as messy as wet plates. They also let photographers develop pictures hours or days after they were taken.

FACT!

Photographer Matthew Brady used wet-plate cameras to take pictures of Civil War battlefields.

15

Chapter 4

The Camera Becomes Popular

The first cameras were expensive, large, and hard to use. Only skilled photographers could take good pictures. Over time, cameras became cheaper and easier to use.

Eastman and the Kodak Camera

In the 1880s, George Eastman made the camera easier for everyone to use. He made film. Unlike heavy plates used in early cameras, his film was flexible. It could be rolled and carried inside the camera. A person could take several pictures before developing the film.

George Eastman takes a
picture with his Kodak camera.

Eastman made the Kodak camera to hold his new film. This small box camera could be held in one hand. It carried a roll of film that could take 100 pictures. The customer mailed the camera back to the factory for photo developing. New film was put in the camera at the factory. Then the camera and the pictures were sent back to the customer.

The back of a Kodak camera slid out so new film could be loaded in. The camera held a roll of film that could take 100 pictures. ▼

In 1900, the Kodak Brownie was introduced. This camera was made for children. It sold for just one dollar. It quickly became popular with adults, too.

35-Millimeter Film

Before 1925, most film was 70 millimeters (2.76 inches) wide. In 1925, Oskar Barnack introduced the Leica camera. The Leica was the first camera to use 35-millimeter (mm) film. This film was cut into strips 35 millimeters (1.38 inches) wide. Smaller film led to smaller cameras. Most cameras today still use 35 mm film.

FACT!

Kodak introduced 35 mm Kodacolor film in 1942. It was the first color negative film for cameras.

▲ The Polaroid 95
Land Camera
was the first
instant camera.

Polaroid

In 1948, Edwin Land made the world's first instant camera. The Polaroid 95 Land Camera was able to develop a picture in just 60 seconds.

The first Polaroid cameras developed pictures inside the camera. In 1972, the Polaroid company began selling the SX-70 Land Camera. It made color prints that developed in full sunlight.

Automatic Cameras

The first automatic cameras were made in the late 1970s. In 1977, the Konica company introduced the Konica C35AF 35 mm camera. It had automatic focus. This feature let the camera focus the lens by itself. Other automatic features for cameras soon followed. Today, cameras have automatic film winding and automatic flash features.

The Konica C35AF was the first camera to use an automatic focus lens. ▼

Chapter 5

How Film Cameras Work

Cameras take pictures by capturing light. All film cameras work in the same basic way. They use a lens, an aperture, a **shutter**, and a closed box to take pictures.

Taking a Picture

A camera uses a lens to gather light reflecting off objects. A lens is a curved piece of glass or plastic. The curve of the lens bends light to a clear focus.

An aperture and a shutter work behind the lens. The aperture is a small hole that controls the amount of light entering the camera. The shutter is a door that opens and closes. It lets light hit the film inside the closed box.

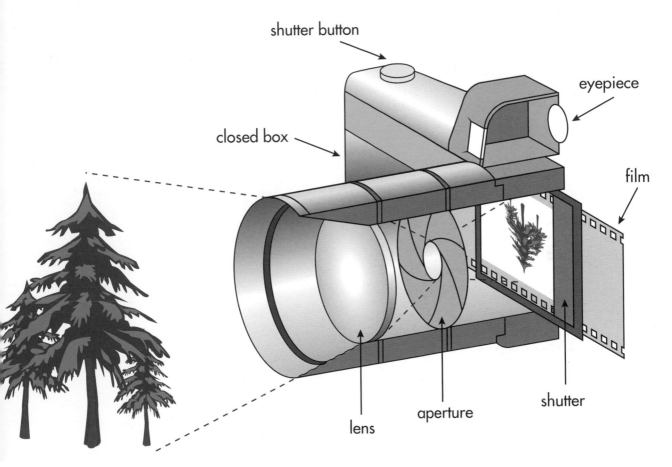

shutter button

eyepiece

closed box

film

lens

aperture

shutter

▲ A camera forms an upside down and backward image on the film when a picture is taken.

When a person takes a picture, the shutter quickly opens. Light enters the closed box. Then the shutter closes. The light that hits the film reacts with chemicals. An image forms on the film.

Chapter 6

Cameras Today

Cameras have continued to change over the years. They are smaller and easier to use than early models. Today, hundreds of models are available in stores. Single-use cameras and digital cameras are two popular styles.

Single-Use Cameras

In 1986, the Fuji Company made the first single-use cameras. These plastic cameras include one roll of film. They use plastic lenses. After the film is used up, the camera is sent to the photo processor for developing. The camera's parts are reused or recycled.

Single-use cameras are easy
for people of all ages to use.

Digital Cameras

In 1990, people began using the first digital cameras. These cameras do not use film. They capture images electronically.

Digital cameras store the images on chips, memory cards, or discs. People can look at the pictures on computers. Digital pictures can be easily sent and shared over the Internet.

Cameras through the Years

Daguerreotype

1837

Anthony & Scovill

1903

Kodak Brown

1929

Lasting Importance

The invention of the camera changed the world. Cameras let people capture real images of the places and people around them. Today, cameras remain an important part of daily life. They let people share news of events around the world. They also help people record important moments in their lives.

Bell & Howell Dial 35

1963

Polaroid OneStep

1977

Olympus Digital Camera

2003

Fast Facts

- Ancient Greeks invented the camera obscura. They used it to project images on the wall of a dark room.

- In 1558, Giambattista della Porta put the first lens in a camera obscura. The lens focused images.

- In 1827, Joseph N. Niepce took the first known photograph. He called his picture a heliograph. The picture showed a scene outside his studio.

- Louis Daguerre invented the daguerreotype camera in 1837.

- In 1900, the Kodak Brownie was introduced. The Brownie was meant for kids, but it became popular with adults.

- Edwin Land introduced the Polaroid 95 in 1948. It was the world's first instant camera.

- In 1986, the Fuji Company made the first single-use camera. Parts from these cameras are reused.

- In 1990, people began using digital cameras.

Hands On: Camera Obscura

The camera obscura was an artist's tool for hundreds of years. It helped artists trace over images to create more lifelike portraits. You can make a camera obscura with a few simple materials. Ask an adult to help you with this activity.

What You Need

small tea box

pencil

ruler

scissors

black paint

paintbrush

tape

tracing paper

What You Do

1. On one end of the tea box, draw a square that has 2-inch (5-centimeter) sides. Use a scissors to cut along the lines of your square. Remove the square.
2. Paint the inside of the box black. Allow the paint to dry.
3. On the outside of the box, tape a piece of tracing paper over the square hole you cut in the box.
4. Use a pencil to poke a small hole in the side of the box opposite the tracing paper.
5. Point the end of the box with the pencil hole toward a bright object. Look at the image of the object that appears on the tracing paper.

Glossary

camera obscura (KAM-ur-uh uhb-SKYOO-rah)—a dark room or box that allows light from a tiny hole to form an image on the opposite wall or side

collodion (kuh-LOH-dee-uhn)—a thick, sticky liquid used to hold light-sensitive materials on wet plates

diorama (dye-oh-RAM-ah)—a huge painting on cloth that was lit from behind

gelatin (JEL-uh-tuhn)—a clear substance made from bones and animal tissue; gelatin was used to hold light-sensitive materials on dry plates.

negative image (NEG-uh-tiv IM-ij)—an image that shows light areas as dark and dark areas as light

photochemical (foh-toh-KEM-i-kuhl)—a mixture of chemicals that are sensitive to light

shutter (SHUHT-ur)—the part of a camera that opens to expose film to light when a picture is taken

Internet Sites

FactHound offers a safe, fun way to find Internet sites related to this book. All of the sites on FactHound have been researched by our staff.

Here's how:
1. Visit *www.facthound.com*
2. Type in this special code **0736826696** for age-appropriate sites. Or enter a search word related to this book for a more general search.
3. Click on the **Fetch It** button.

FactHound will fetch the best sites for you!

Read More

Bankston, John. *Louis Daguerre and the First Photograph.* Uncharted, Unexplored, and Unexplained. Hockessin, Del.: Mitchell Lane Publishers, 2004.

Ford, Carin T. *George Eastman: The Kodak Camera Man.* Famous Inventors. Berkeley Heights, N.J.: Enslow, 2003.

Wallace, Joseph E. *The Camera.* Turning Point Inventions. New York: Atheneum Books for Young Readers, 2000.

Index